Johnson's Emotional First Aid

To Amy Elizabeth Gilmore
A loving and wise Ms. Thera Peutic
Who is filled with ahas and ha-has

Acknowledgments

I lovingly thank and acknowledge those who were helpful in many important ways. I'm grateful to Joseph Iasiello, a dear friend, who first encouraged me to write this book, and very appreciative to Cass Kocak, a gifted artist, for putting Ms. Thera Peutic on paper and for her great creative touch with the illustrations and design.

Lydia Iasiello, a wonderful friend, helped in many ways, including editing, feedback, and generous loving support. Joyce Corinna, with her numerous talents, was helpful with her editorial and artistic advice and loving encouragement. I'm thankful to Lee Doyal, an outstanding mental health counselor, for her professional expertise, editorial help, and heart-to-heart encouragement. Mary Ann Gibavitch lovingly shared information and her invaluable editing expertise. Nancy Shirley enlivened Ms. Thera Peutic with special color, Laura Pike and David Reierson added their color skills and generous help. Kimberly Grzech creatively brought all of the parts together.

I'm grateful to Nancy and Paul Clemens, who have a big vision and high purpose, and to everyone at Blue Dolphin Publishing for their knowledge, skills, and final loving touches with *Johnson's Emotional First Aid*.

Pauline Flynn's unfailing love and support for all I do is a precious gift. I am deeply appreciative to my dear family, friends, and clients with whom I had many of the insights I included in this book. A great big THANK YOU to all others who helped in various ways.

CONTENTS

I. Emotional First Aid Suggestions

Affirmation 12
Anger 14
Anxiety 16, 30
Awareness . . . . .18 & every page
Calm .54, 59, 37
Change 19, 57, 63
Confusion 18, 46
Courage 20
Criticism .21, 61
Depression 22, 64, 14, 53, 52, 44, 56
Despair 23, 28, 42, 40, 53, 22
Encourage .20, 61
Emptiness 5, 52, 65, 40, 51
Emotion 24, 44, 54, 66
Endurance 26, 44, 28
Faith .28, 42, 40
Fear .30, 16, 20, 28
Forgiveness 31, 63
Gratefulness 25
Grief 33, 56, 52, 64, 40, 57
Guilt 35, 31
Happiness 37, 49, 52, 65, 45, 61
Harm 38
Harmony 38, 37, 52, 59
Higher Power 40, 52
Hope 42, 65, 12, 28
Hugs 44
Humor 45
Insecurity 66, 30, 16, 19, 20, 12
Insigh 46, 18
Jealous 47, 66
Joy 49, 52, 37
Loneliness 51, 52, 65, 53, 37, 44
Love 52, 49
Loss 64, 33, 19, 56, 57, 63
Low 53, 52, 40, 61
Meditation 54
Mourning 56, 33, 64, 26, 57
Peace 59, 54
Praise 61
Present 62
Regret 35, 31, 63, 62
Relaxation 54
Release 63, 19, 57
Sadness 64, 52, 24
Sorrow 64, 52, 33, 56, 63
Stress 54, 59, 37, 45, 49
Unhappiness 37, 53, 25, 52, 44, 49, 45
Visualize 65
Wholeness .66, 37
Worry 30, 16, 24, 28, 40

II. Emotional First Aid Topics

Introduction 11
Affirmation 12
Anger 14
Anxiety 16
Awareness 18
Change 19
Courage 20
Criticize 21
Depression 22
Despair 23
Emotion 24
Empty 25
Endure 26
Faith 28
Fear 30
Forgive 31
Grief 33
Guilt 35
Happiness 37
Harmony 38
Higher Power 40
Hope 42
Hugs 44
Humor 45
Insight 46
Jealousy 47
Joy 49
Lonely 51
Love 52
Low — Hi! 53
Meditate 54
Mourning 56
News 57
Peace 59
Praise 61
Present 62
Release 63
Sadness 64
Visualize 65
Whole 66
Write It Out 68

Preface

Johnson's Emotional First Aid, like physical first aid books, provides handy and immediate assistance to either alleviate your problem or to aid you until you can obtain professional help. This book has valuable suggestions for when you feel sad, angry, anxious, or need help with other emotional conditions. There are many ideas to read and use any time for increasing your happiness, peace, and joy.

If your symptoms are more than moderate, or if you have felt them longer than just recently, I urge you to seek professional help quickly. These emotional first aid suggestions are not intended to replace the services of psychological professionals.

This book is also intended for you to use to educate yourself about your emotions and the emotions of other people. Although emotions are felt daily, there is little education pertaining to emotions. As a marriage and family therapist, I find that numerous people simply need to be educated to know what to do when they or other people feel emotional.

Many difficulties could be prevented by education. For example: Parents brought in their teenage son for a therapy session because he was very angry with his father. "He doesn't care about me," the son yelled angrily. The father angrily replied, "How can you say that, with all I do for you?" The father loved his son and expressed it by giving him things, but he did not know how to express his love in a way his son could hear and feel.

I have heard the following statements many times. Perhaps you, too, have said, thought, or heard them. "I was so upset, I could not think straight." "I did not know what to say or do to help." Many people are overwhelmed when they feel emotional or someone else feels emotional. No matter what age you are, you may suddenly feel like a child who does not know what to do. Even if you do know, it may not be in a succinct, easily remembered, and quickly useable form.

Children and adults learn and remember best when information is presented in a short, simple form, and from what they see adults do. This is the reason for the simple headings on the pages, such as "Sadness Out, Love and Kindness In," and illustrations where you can see the cartoon character presenting the emotion and the solution. *Johnson's Emotional First Aid* presents therapeutically sound educational information in a style and form to help you learn, and to remember what you have learned, when you need it the most.

I use a variety of therapeutic techniques when I work as a marriage and family therapist with clients, as well as when I write. Some are for the conscious and subconscious mind, and others are for the emotions. Some methods invoke the child, adult, and parent ego states, and others utilize the functions of the left and right brain. Blending seriousness and humor, I integrate work with play. I believe in playfully combining ahas and ha-has and created cartoon character Ms. Thera Peutic as an amusing and insightful guide.

I have found in my therapy sessions and in my writing that the greatest benefits occur when the abstract is made concrete, and the complex is made simple. I believe simplicity and simple truths can be profound. For example: A client started crying as soon as she arrived. She tearfully talked about what was happening in her life. I listened. When she finished speaking, I wrote the words Mourning and Morning on my large pad and drew a sun. I watched as a light seemed to suddenly shine from her face. She smiled. She looked relieved. She was mourning an ending and loss, and she had not yet realized the possibility of a gain and new beginning.

I decided to write this book after many clients reported carrying over these simple solutions from our sessions into their everyday lives, because they were easily understood, remembered, and applied. I heard similar reports from people who were not my clients, but had attended my lectures when I presented the words and illustrations on slides.

This book is also intended for you to use therapeutically, if you need only a minimum amount of help, or if you are a person who insists on doing it for yourself, by yourself. Clients usually begin psychotherapy sessions with upsetting emotions and thoughts. We work together towards a resolution of awareness, alternatives, and action. You can work on taking yourself from your upsetting emotions and thoughts towards your desired outcome by using this book as a workbook. Awareness, specific alternatives, and the action you can take are included for each emotional topic. You can also use it in conjunction with psychotherapy by working through it with your therapist.

When I was a student intern working with my first client, I felt a sense of awe for the sacredness of being with her as she opened her feelings and thoughts to herself and to me, while I lovingly listened. Over the twenty years since, I have continued to feel a sacred trust for this privilege. As I write now, I wonder about you, who you are, and what your needs are as you read my words and see the illustrations. I have written this book with the knowledge, insights, and wisdom from my many years of education and experience, and most importantly, I have written it with love. I hope that you will benefit greatly from reading and applying these emotional first aid suggestions. Enjoy!

— Victoria Ann Johnson

INTRODUCTION

HI!

I'm Ms. Thera Peutic,
Your friendly, playful nurse,
Here to help you
With pictures, words, and verse.
But there's only so much I can do.
The action and results
Are up to you.

So, come into my book
And follow me through,
To find out all that you can do.

Affirmation

Affirm
A Firm Foundation

Do you want A FIRM FOUNDATION?

1. AFFIRMATIONS are quality ideas about yourself and life that can become statements of fact.

2. Many beliefs about yourself and your life were formed unconsciously during childhood. Often based on misperceptions and other people's attitudes and actions, they may have created an unstable, shaky, belief system foundation. Your beliefs may not match your adult reality.

3. Write AFFIRMATIONS to create A FIRM, new, positive, belief system FOUNDATION.

a. Write a statement about yourself or your life that you want to have as a statement of fact. Make it positive and in the present, as if it already were a fact.

b. Next, write down any negative thoughts and feelings you have about your AFFIRMATION.

c. Then rewrite your AFFIRMATION adding or deleting words until you can accept it and feel good about it.

d. Write your AFFIRMATION several times. If you have any negative thoughts or feelings repeat suggestions b. and c. from above.

e. Repeat the above process until you can think, verbalize, and write your AFFIRMATION without negative feelings and thoughts.

f. Write AFFIRMATIONS for any positive change you want in yourself and in your life.

4. Write, verbalize, and silently repeat your AFFIRMATIONS daily for at least thirty days. Silently repeat them whenever you have a negative thought or feeling contrary to the AFFIRMATIONS.

5. Make a tape recording of your AFFIRMATIONS. You may want to use background music. Repeat your AFFIRMATIONS several times.

6. It can be helpful to record each AFFIRMATION three ways.

a. Begin by saying, "I, _____ (your name)," and then repeat your AFFIRMATION.

b. Next, begin with "You, _____ (your name)," and repeat your AFFIRMATION as if someone were talking to you.

c. Complete your recording with "She, _____ (your name)," and repeat your AFFIRMATION as if someone were talking about you and you were listening.

Anger

Stop

Take Constructive Action

STOP! TAKE CONSTRUCTIVE ACTION

1. Whenever you feel ANGRY, you want something to be different than it is. You may be able to go directly from feeling ANGRY to CONSTRUCTIVE ACTION by using #2 below. Or you may need to decrease your ANGER before you can think of CONSTRUCTIVE ACTION, especially if you feel a lot of ANGER or have unexpressed ANGER from similar circumstances in the past. If so, use #3 in next column.

2. You feel ANGRY.

   a. <u>Stop!</u>

   b. <u>Think!</u>

   c. <u>Ask</u> yourself,

   "What do I want to be different?"

   "What can I do to make it be different?"

d. <u>Act</u> when you decide on CONSTRUCTIVE ACTION.

3. You feel ANGRY.

   a. <u>Stop!</u>

   b. <u>Decrease</u> your ANGER. See #4 below.

   c. <u>Think!</u>

   d. <u>Ask</u> yourself,

   "What do I want to be different?"

   "What can I do to make it be different?"

   e. <u>Act</u> when you decide on CONSTRUCTIVE ACTION.

4. When you feel a lot of ANGER, you feel a lot of energy and want to do something with that energy. You may be able to decrease your ANGER by using the following suggestions.

14

a. Do a physical activity such as walking briskly, yard work, house cleaning, or a sport.

b. Distract yourself with other things and let time pass.

5. Sometimes having CONSTRUCTIVE ways to express your ANGER, can be helpful.

 a. Talk it out with another person. Ask them to simply listen without judging you. Tell them not to give you advice or to try to solve your problem. Do not direct your ANGER at them. Tell them about your ANGER.

 b. Write out everything you are feeling. Do not judge your feelings. If your feelings involve another person write them a letter. This is for your benefit. Express whatever you want to express, and then tear it up and throw it away.

 c. Express it safely and constructively to the person towards whom you feel ANGER. Do not verbally or physically attack them. It usually is best to wait until you feel less ANGER and can communicate better. Stay focused on one issue. Briefly state your perception of what happened. Express your feelings using "I feel _____" statements. Take responsibility for your feelings. Say what you want to have happen.

 d. Express it verbally and physically in a safe, indirect way. Pretend a pillow is the person towards whom you feel ANGER, or the thing you are ANGRY about. You can shake, punch, or kick the pillow as you verbally express your feelings.

6. Understanding your ANGER may help you decrease it. It can be a response to a present situation or from another recent or long ago situation.

 a. Ask yourself, "What am I really ANGRY about?"

 b. Write down everything that comes to your mind.

7. If you repeatedly feel ANGRY in similar situations, even though the people involved may be different, feel more ANGER than present circumstances warrant, and feel powerless to do anything, your ANGER may be from the past.

 a. Make a list of the times and situations when you responded with ANGER. Find the similarities.

 b. Did you have similar situations and feelings in childhood? If so, go back to the earliest time you remember and safely and CONSTRUCTIVELY express your feelings now. See #5 above.

 c. Afterwards close your eyes and recreate that situation in your imagination the way you wanted it to be.

8. You may be able to decrease your ANGER in your present situation by understanding the other person.

 a. If there were present or past circumstances which affected the other person's actions, what do you think they might have been?

 b. Can you decrease your ANGER by having understanding and consideration for that person?

9. TAKE CONSTRUCTIVE ACTION.

 a. Are there internal changes you can make within yourself, and external changes you can make in your environment?

 b. Write down what you want to do that will benefit you and not harm you or another person. Make an action plan of how, when, and where you will do it, and then TAKE CONSTRUCTIVE ACTION.

Anxiety and Action

1. ANXIETY is fear without a specific focus for the fear. It is often fear of feeling, expressing, and acting on your own emotions.

   a. Read this book and others to learn about emotions and how to express them in healthy, productive ways.

   b. Talk to an understanding, compassionate, non-judgmental listener and share your feelings and thoughts. Professional help can be beneficial.

2. ANXIETY can sometimes be helped by taking care of your physical body.

   a. Do not skip meals. Eat a balanced diet.

   b. Choose an exercise or sport you enjoy and do it daily, or at least three times a week.

   c. Have a medical and nutritional checkup to find out if a physical condition is causing or contributing to the ANXIETY.

   d. Meditate daily. See Meditate, p. 54.

   e. Relax. Do what helps you relax, or use a relaxation tape.

3. ANXIETY is usually based on past experiences and future fears, and often decreases when you focus on the present.

   a. Focus outward rather than inward on yourself. Use your eyes and ears to see and hear other people and your surroundings. Focus on how they are, not on how you think they are viewing you.

   b. See Present, p. 62.

4. If you attempt to focus outward and have difficulty focusing on anything but yourself, focus on your breathing.

   a. Breathe long, slow, deep breaths. Focus your mind on your body's rhythmic inhales and exhales. You may begin to yawn. Good! This is a sign you are relaxing.

   b. Calm your emotions by making your exhales twice as long as your inhales.

5. Combine breathing with visualization.

   a. Choose a symbol that represents peace, such as a calm lake.

   b. Visualize your symbol while you breathe long, slow, deep breaths.

   c. Imagine you breathe in peace as you inhale, and you

breathe out ANXIETY as you exhale.

   d. Listen to a relaxation audio tape and follow the guided visualization.

6. When you feel ANXIETY about something you are going to do in the future, you probably imagine terrible things are going to happen. Choose instead to use your imagination in a positive way.

   a. Close your eyes. Take three long, slow, deep breaths. As you inhale say to yourself, "I am," and as you exhale say to yourself, "relaxed." Focus on your breathing.

   b. When you feel relaxed, visualize yourself confidently doing what you need to do. Use all your senses to fully imagine your future experience exactly as you want it to be.

7. Feeling ANXIETY is often compared to feeling like a frightened, powerless child. Use the adult part of you to comfort and care for the child within you.

   a. A frightened child wants a hand to hold. Pretend your one hand is the hand of your frightened child and your other hand is the hand of your adult. Use your adult hand to hold, stroke, and nurture your child hand.

   b. Talk to yourself with reassuring parental words. "I'm here with you. I'll take care of you. You'll be alright."

   c. If you cannot comfort yourself, use your inner adult to choose someone to help you. Ask someone with whom you can be your frightened inner child.

8. Having too much or too little control in childhood can contribute to adult ANXIETY and confusion about control.

   a. Think about and write down under what circumstances you feel ANXIETY.

   b. Remember if you had emotionally similar experiences in childhood. If so, did you feel powerless then to make things be different than they were? See Whole, p. 66.

   c. Do you feel ANXIOUS and powerless in similar circumstances now, even though you do have power but do not use it to make things be different than they are?

9. When you feel ANXIETY, do you feel as if you have no control?

   a. Make a list of what you feel you can and cannot control.

   b. Rationally think about each item on your list.

   c. Decide what you can do to have and use more power and control in your life.

   d. Take ACTION.

10. ACTION is a remedy for ANXIETY. When you feel ANXIETY, do you withdraw and do less? Do more!

   a. Daily increase your activities and interactions with other people.

   b. If you feel overwhelmed doing this, do it little by little. Concentrate on doing what you are doing, and then do what needs to be done next.

   c. Praise and reward yourself for each ACTION.

Awareness,
Alternatives,
and Action

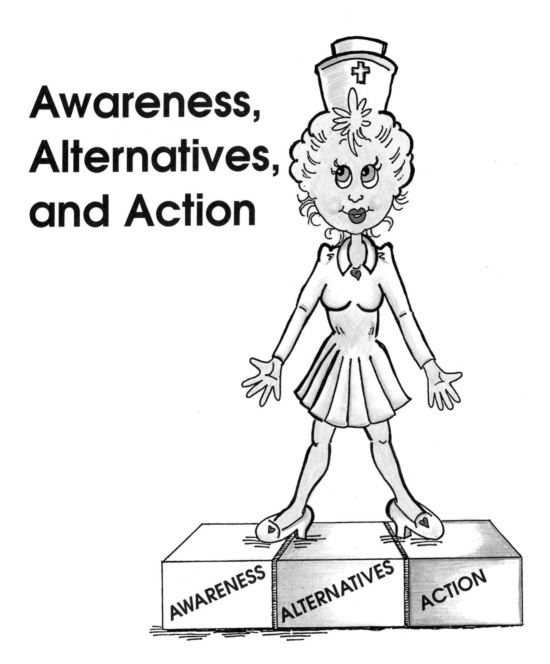

Are you feeling confused and need "under-standing?" Do you have a problem and need a solution?

Ask yourself:
1. "What am I AWARE of?"
2. "What are my ALTERNATIVES?"
3. "What ACTION will I take?"

Change

A Change is an Exchange.

1. Write the word CHANGE at the top of a blank piece of paper and write down everything that comes to your mind when you think of CHANGE.

   a. Did you include positive and negative things and words of loss and words of gain?

   b. Often CHANGE is feared because of fear of loss, and the positive gain is overlooked.

2. There are chosen CHANGES and unchosen CHANGES.

   a. In a chosen CHANGE the gain is usually emphasized and felt first, and the loss is felt later.

   b. In an unchosen CHANGE the loss is often focused on first, and the gain is felt later.

Exchange

3. Have you recently gone through a CHANGE, or will you soon be going through one?

   a. Make a list of what you keep, what you lose, and what you gain.

   b. Make a list of EXCHANGES. I exchange _____ for _____.

4. The most difficult stage of a CHANGE is when you had a loss and have not yet received your gain.

   a. During this time it is helpful to know all CHANGE is an EXCHANGE.

   b. Grieve your loss. See Grief, p. 33.

   c. Think about, write down, and do what is necessary to give yourself the gain from your CHANGE.

19

Courage

ENCOURAGE for COURAGE!

1. Life is filled with acts of COURAGE. They involve a risk, sometimes fear, and going beyond the risk and fear. Standing upright on your own two feet for the first time was a major act of COURAGE.

   a. Make a list of all your COURAGEOUS acts. Include the recent, long ago, large, and small.

   b. Most acts of COURAGE have inner and possibly outer gifts. Increased self-love is often one of them. Next to each act of COURAGE on your COURAGE list write the gifts you received.

2. What was the most COURAGEOUS thing you have done? Tell someone about it.

3. Many acts of COURAGE had prior ENCOURAGEMENT. Hearten and cheer are synonyms for ENCOURAGE.

4. Your first baby steps were lovingly ENCOURAGED by an adult. Now you can ENCOURAGE yourself, be ENCOURAGED by others, and ENCOURAGE others.

   a. Write a letter of ENCOURAGEMENT to yourself. Begin with "Dear (your name), I ENCOURAGE you to," and write praise and ENCOURAGEMENT to yourself. Read it daily.

   b. Give a gift of an ENCOURAGING letter or phone call to someone who needs it.

   c. Have an "ENCOURAGEMENT Partnership" with someone. Tell them how they can ENCOURAGE you, and ask them how you can ENCOURAGE them.

Encourage

Criticize

Criti - Size

When you are CRITICIZED or CRITICIZE, do you feel reduced in size?

1. CRITICISM reduces feelings of love and self-esteem. It can make you feel you are less than who you truly are. If you CRITICIZE yourself or are CRITICIZED frequently, you may begin to believe and act like you are that way.

2. What do you use CRITICISM of yourself and others for? It is used to punish, to motivate, to exercise power over others, and to raise yourself by lowering someone else.

   a. If you punish yourself with CRITICISM, instead ask yourself, "How can I use this to improve myself?" And, "What can I learn from this?"

   b. If you punish others with CRITICISM when you are angry, instead express how you feel, and ask for what you want.

   c. Motivate yourself and others with praise. When you realize you CRITICIZED yourself, praise yourself.

   d. Use power over yourself, not over another person. Change your behavior, not their behavior.

   e. Raise yourself by praising yourself and other people.

3. The following will help you realize how much you CRITICIZE and praise yourself, and to physically feel the emotional impact of praise and CRITICISM.

   a. Wear an elastic band on your wrist for a day.

   b. Lovingly pat your wrist when you praise yourself, and snap the elastic band when you CRITICIZE yourself.

4. When you are CRITICIZED, do you react emotionally?

   a. Remember that a CRITICISM is only one person's opinion, and CRITICISM usually says more about the speaker than about the person CRITICIZED.

   b. If you do not want to listen to CRITICISM, tell the person, "I feel CRITICIZED. I do not want to be CRITICIZED. If you have something to say to me, say it in a positive way."

   c. If you must listen to CRITICISM, listen with your mind, not your emotions. Ask yourself, "Does this say more about the speaker than about me?" And, "Is there something valid being said that can help me?"

5. If you must judge other people, judge their behavior or product, not the person. Find what you can praise in them, even if you are CRITICAL of the behavior or product.

6. Be aware of how you feel about yourself, and the feelings others express towards you, when you CRITICIZE or praise yourself and others.

CRITI □ size

21

Expression

Depression

Feeling DEPRESSED? EXPRESS your feelings!

1. Talk them out with a compassionate, non-judgmental listener. Ask them to simply listen and not to try to solve your problems or give you advice.

2. Write them out.

   a. Write everything you are feeling. You can write it out on p.68 at the back of this book. Do not judge your feelings.

   b. If your feelings involve another person, write them a letter. This is for your benefit, not to give to the other person. EXPRESS all your true feelings, and then tear it up, throw it away, or burn it.

3. EXPRESS them verbally or physically in a safe way.

   a. Pretend a pillow is the person towards whom you feel anger or sadness.

   b. You can punch, cry on, or hug the pillow as you verbally EXPRESS to that person.

4. Tell the person directly how you are feeling. Use "I feel _____ " statements. See Anger, p. 14.

5. Do something loving and kind for yourself. If you do not know what to do, do for yourself what you would do for a sad child or a friend who feels the way you feel.

6. Tell someone how you are feeling and ask them to do something loving and kind for you.

7. Be touched. Ask for a hug, a back rub, a massage, or get a professional massage from a caring massage therapist.

8. If you continue to feel DEPRESSED or have felt DEPRESSED for awhile, have a medical and nutritional checkup to determine if there is a physical cause.

Despair   # Repair

Feeling DESPAIR? REPAIR!

1. Do something that would be good for you, and would make you feel a little better now. If you do not know what to do, do for yourself what you would do for a sad child, or a friend who feels the way you feel.

2. Ask for help and emotional support from your family and friends.

3. Find at least one person to talk to about your feelings and thoughts. Choose someone who is compassionate, loving, and non-judgmental. Professional help can be beneficial.

4. Find a picture or a symbolic representation of the way you want to feel, and place it where you will see it often. Fill yourself with those feelings.

5. Write a list of your resources. List personal qualities, education, experiences, accomplishments, work experience, financial assets and possessions, interpersonal relationships, and religious, educational, community, state, and national resources.

6. Decide what you need to do, how to best use resources, and make an action plan. Be specific with how, when, and where you will do your action and then do it.

7. Do something good for yourself every day. Each night write down what you did for yourself that day, and what you did from your action plan.

Emotion   # No Motion

Motion

Feeling too much EMOTION?

1. Do you feel too much EMOTION from not doing enough MOTION? EMOTIONS are sometimes calmed through physical MOTION.

   a. When you are EMOTIONALLY upset, calm yourself by walking briskly or doing a task-oriented physical activity such as house cleaning, gardening, or home repairs.

   b. Choose an exercise or sport you enjoy and do it daily or at least three times a week.

   c. Do a calming walk by inhaling through your nose with a long, slow, deep breath as you take two long walking strides forward. Exhale through your mouth with a long, slow, deep breath as you take four long walking strides forward. Taking twice the length of time and number of strides to exhale as to inhale is calming.

   d. Think about and write down what you want or need to do that you have delayed or avoided. Write down the final outcomes you hope for, and what you fear might happen.

   e. Decide what you will do, and how, when, and where you will do it. And then put your action plan and yourself into MOTION.

2. Do you feel EMOTIONALLY upset from too much activity? EMOTIONS are sometimes calmed by NO MOTION.

   a. Sit in a quiet, comfortable place. Close your eyes. Breathe long, slow, deep breaths. Sit quietly and silently for awhile.

   b. Give yourself time to do nothing. Begin today with at least one hour, and make it a day as soon as you can.

   c. Learn meditation and do it daily. See Meditate, p. 54.

   d. Think about how you use your time, and what you can eliminate, decrease, or delegate to others.

   e. Make decisions of what you will and will not do and act on your decisions.

Empty

Grateful

Feeling EMPTY? Want to feel full?
Be GRATEFUL!

1. Close your eyes. Take a few long, slow, deep breaths. Silently or verbally say to yourself, "I'm thankful for _____," and say everyone and everything that comes to your mind. Fill yourself with your loving and GRATEFUL feelings. Be aware of how you feel when you finish, compared to how you feel when you begin.

2. Write a list of everything you are thankful for. Include the small, the ordinary, and the major things. Do this every day for a week and for greatest results continue indefinitely.

3. It can be helpful to label a notebook, "My GREAT FULLNESS Book." Whatever you concentrate on increases. Concentrate on and increase your GRATEFULNESS.

4. Write a thank you letter to yourself. Begin with "Dear (your name), I thank you for _____," and write everything that comes to your mind.

5. Write thank you letters and make thank you phone calls to other people for their recent and long-ago gifts.

Endure

End Door/
Beginning Door

End Door/Beginning Door

1. Sometimes there are difficulties that you cannot change, that you must accept and ENDURE.

    a. Change what you can change.

    b. If you cannot change what you want to change, find something over which you do have power and control and change that.

    c. Accept what you cannot change. If you cannot do that now, be patient with yourself and give yourself time to do so.

2. A support system can help you ENDURE.

    a. Ask your family and friends for help and emotional support.

    b. Talk to someone and express your feelings and thoughts. Choose someone who is a compassionate, loving, non-judgmental listener. Professional help can be beneficial.

    c. Attend support group meetings for people with challenges. Call the Mental Health Association, churches, synagogues, hospitals, counseling centers, and schools for information.

3. Nurture yourself.

   a. Do something good for yourself that would make you feel a little better now. If you do not know what to do, think of what you would do for an unhappy child or a friend who feels as you do. Do that for yourself.

   b. Do something good for yourself every day. Each night write down what you did that day.

   c. Be easy on yourself.

   d. Eat healthy, balanced meals and do an exercise or a sport you enjoy.

   e. Be outdoors in nature. Nature is always changing, and there is an ENDURANCE and strength in nature that can help and strengthen you.

   f. Remind yourself you haven't always felt this way, and you will not always feel this way in the future.

4. Belief in a Higher Power can help you ENDURE, whether it is in a religious, spiritual, mythological, nature, or metaphysical form, or is formless.

   a. Do you believe in a Higher Power? If so, ask your Higher Power for help.

   b. See Higher Power, p. 40.

5. ENDURE by simply doing what needs to be done next. ENDURE hour by hour, day by day.

6. Know that at times you will probably feel sad, angry, weak, and lonely, and other times you will begin to feel stronger and able to go forward.

   a. Accept how you feel.

   b. Be with people who love and accept you as you are.

7. Be thankful for the "little things." At the end of each day say to yourself, "I'm thankful for _____," and name everything you are thankful for.

8. Know that all things change eventually. When you ENDURE, you will get to an END DOOR/BEGINNING DOOR.

   a. What new BEGINNING do you want on the other side of your END DOOR?

   b. What can you do to get there more quickly?

   c. Happily anticipate and plan for your new BEGINNING.

   d. See Visualize, Visual Eyes, p. 65.

9. What inner gifts are you discovering and developing within yourself during your time of ENDURING? Great strength can come from knowing you can ENDURE. Decide on a special gift and give it to yourself when you get to your END DOOR/BEGINNING DOOR.

Faith & Action

Do you want to have FAITH?

1. FAITH is belief and trust before you have evidence and proof, and ACTION to actualize what you want.

    a. What do you want? Write it down. Leave blank lines between the items.

    b. Write down on the blank lines what ACTION you can do to reach your goals.

2. What assets do you have that can help you reach your goals? Write down your personal qualities, knowledge, experience, accomplishments, interpersonal relationships, and other assets.

3. Give your goal a symbolic form before it is a reality.

    a. Find, cut out, and paste words and pictures that represent what you want on a large sheet of paper or poster board. Place it where you see it often, and fill yourself with the good feelings of having what you want.

    b. Carry a small symbol of your goal with you at all times.

4. Strengthen your FAITH by listing all the times you had problems or challenges and had the outcomes you wanted.

5. Read FAITH-filled articles, stories, and biographies of people who overcame adversities and actualized their potentials through FAITH and ACTION.

6. Encouragement and support from other people can help you have FAITH.

   a. Have "FAITH Friends." Find others who had similar circumstances and happy outcomes. Learn what they did and how they did it. Ask them to help you have FAITH, to be your "FAITH Friend."

   b. Start a "FAITH Group" with other people. Meet once a week. Focus on how you want things to be. Discuss what you are doing to make your goals become realities. Encourage each other to go forward, have FAITH, and take ACTION.

   c. Attend support group meetings. Call the Mental Health Association, counseling centers, hospitals, churches, synagogues, or schools for information.

7. Belief in a Higher Power is beneficial for FAITH, whether it is in a religious, spiritual, metaphysical, nature, or mythological form, or is formless.

   a. Do you believe in a Higher Power? If so, ask your Higher Power for help.

   b. See Higher Power, p. 40.

8. Adult FAITH or absence of FAITH can unconsciously go back to childhood.

   a. When you were a child, did you get what you wanted more often than not? If not, do you believe you can't get what you want, and can't give it to yourself?

   b. Do your beliefs match your present adult reality, or are you acting as if you can't give yourself what you want, when you can?

   c. Think of something you wanted and did not receive when you were a child. Give it to yourself now in reality, in imagination, or in another form.

9. Give something to yourself you now want. Fill yourself with the good feelings of having what you want, and the powerful feeling of giving it to yourself.

10. Increase your FAITH by having a positive perception of the times you did not get what you wanted.

    a. Think of those times now.

    b. Now choose to think of them in a different way. From an older and wiser viewpoint, can you think of how it may have been good you did not get what you wanted? Did you get something better instead, or did you benefit in another way?

11. Focus on the outcomes you want, not on the problems or challenges. Visualize your desired outcomes. See Visualize, p. 65.

Fear  Face It Go Beyond It

FEAR — FACE IT, and GO BEYOND IT.

1. FEAR is often used to protect, motivate, punish, and control.

   a. Think back to your childhood. Remember how your parents and other people used FEAR.

   b. Now think about how you use FEAR.

2. Write down what you FEAR. You can write it on p. 68 in this book.

   a. Are these your FEARS or FEARS of your parents and other people?

   b. Next to each FEAR write the name of the person who had the FEAR.

3. Are your FEARS based on fact or fallacy? Get the facts about what you FEAR.

4. Write down what you FEARED in the past but no longer FEAR today, and what you did to GO BEYOND the FEAR.

5. Think of the FEARFUL part of yourself as a little child, and another part of yourself as a protective parent.

   a. When you feel FEAR, hold one hand securely in your other hand.

   b. Imagine that your inner parent is taking care of and protecting your inner child.

6. Tell someone about your FEARS. Choose someone who will be nurturing, non-judgmental, and supportive.

7. Make a decision to FACE and GO BEYOND the FEAR.

   a. Decide what you need to do, and how you will reward yourself after you do it.

   b. Visualize yourself FACING and GOING BEYOND the FEAR. Emphasize the positive outcome. See Visualize, p. 65.

   c. Take action and GO BEYOND the FEAR. Joyfully reward yourself when you do!

Can't Forget?

Forgive!

Do you want to FORGIVE and FORGET?

1. FORGIVE other people and FORGIVE yourself for what was done and was not done. FORGIVE yourself for the ways you hurt yourself because of it.

   a. Write down the names of the people you want to FORGIVE and what you want to FORGIVE them for.

   b. What do you want to FORGIVE yourself for? Write it down.

2. Express the emotions you feel towards yourself, the other people, and the events. Use the suggestions for Expression, p. 22, and for the specific emotions you are feeling, such as Sadness, p. 64, Anger, p. 14 , or Guilt, p. 35.

3. Change your perceptions of the people and events. Emotionally motivated thoughts could have distorted your perceptions.

   a. After you express your emotions allow some time to pass, and then think about the people and events again. Focus on understanding the facts in your mind.

   b. Ask yourself, "If I perceived this differently, how could I perceive it?"

   c. You can know what happened and also use your imagination to recreate it a different way. Imagine and recreate it the way you wanted it to be.

   d. You may be able to change your perception, or you may need to accept it as it is.

e. If you repeatedly need to FORGIVE and FORGET in similar situations even though the people may be different each time, you may be repeating patterns from childhood. See suggestions for Whole, p. 66.

4. Feel compassion for yourself and the other people.

a. If you have difficulty feeling compassion, understanding the childhoods can help you feel compassion. It does not excuse the behavior, but it can make it easier to FORGIVE.

b. Imagine you are not an active participant, but a wise and unconditionally loving outside observer. From this viewpoint feel compassion for all who were involved.

c. Close your eyes and breathe three long, slow, deep breaths. Imagine you are surrounded and filled with a brilliant white light of FORGIVENESS. Next, imagine it is surrounding and filling the person you want to FORGIVE.

5. Contact the people you want to have FORGIVE you.

a. Tell them what you regret, and what you wish you did differently. Ask them to FORGIVE you.

b. If it would harm either of you to be in contact, or if you want FORGIVENESS from someone who died, write them a letter, tear it up, and throw it away. Or imagine you speak to them, they answer, and they FORGIVE you.

c. Make amends to other people if you would harm no one to do so.

6. FORGIVENESS is selectively remembering what you want to remember, and choosing what you will FORGET.

a. Make a list of all the times you were proud of yourself for who you were and what you did.

b. Feel thankful for the good things the other people did and the inner and outer gifts you received from them.

7. It can be easier to FORGIVE and FORGET someone if you are meeting the needs you met with them with another person or in another way.

8. Write and verbalize "FORGIVENESS Affirmations" for yourself and others. Use these affirmations or write your own. See Affirmation, p. 12.

a. "I am who I am now. From this wiser and more compassionate me, I begin to understand and have compassion for the me I was then. I now FORGIVE myself."

b. "The wiser and more compassionate me begins to understand and have compassion for _____. I now FORGIVE _____, knowing FORGIVENESS and the peace it brings is a gift I give to myself."

9. Give yourself your gifts. Every experience, no matter how difficult it was, brings gifts.

a. What did you learn? What personality traits did it help you develop?

b. Give yourself a gift of something you would truly enjoy.

Grief

Relief

Do you want RELIEF from your GRIEF?

1. When you GRIEVE, you probably will ask and try to answer three questions.

   a. Could the outcome have been prevented?

   b. Can the outcome be changed?

   c. How can I accept the outcome?

2. A support system is beneficial when you feel GRIEF.

   a. Be with people who love and accept you as you are, and do not try to talk you out of feeling as you feel.

   b. Ask family and friends for help and emotional support.

   c. Talk to a loving, compassionate, non-judgmental listener and share your thoughts and feelings. Professional help can be beneficial.

   d. Attend a support group for people with your challenge. For information call the Mental Health Association, counseling centers, churches, synagogues, or schools.

3. Allow yourself to GRIEVE. At first you may try pretending that what happened did not happen. It is beneficial to move beyond denial and allow yourself to feel and express your emotions. Sadness, anger, and guilt are usually felt when you go from GRIEF to RELIEF.

   a. Express your sadness. See Sadness, p. 64.

   b. You probably will feel angry with the person or thing you lost, and with yourself. See Anger, p. 14.

   c. Are you thinking, "I should have, I shouldn't have, what if..., if only I did, if only I didn't?" See Guilt, p. 35, and Forgive, p. 31.

4. Do you feel as if you are two people? Do you sometimes feel overwhelmed, emotional, and powerless like a child, and other times feel capable, confident, and accepting like an adult?

   a. When you feel like an insecure child, use your inner parent to reassure and nurture yourself, or be with other people and ask for reassurance and nurturing.

   b. The emotions you presently feel may partially be unexpressed emotions from emotionally similar experiences in your childhood. See Whole, p. 66.

   c. You will feel like an adult more of the time, and like a child less of the time, as you feel and express your emotions and take action to move forward.

   d. Your adult will be strengthened by gathering information, knowing the facts, and doing what needs to be done.

5. Acceptance is a final stage of GRIEF.

   a. Admit your loss and move on to meet the needs you met with the person or thing you lost with other people and in other ways.

   b. Did you have a dream, and was the person or thing you lost a part of it? Let go of who or what you lost, keep your dream, and find other ways to fulfill and live it.

   c. Forgiveness is important for acceptance. See Forgive, p. 31.

   d. Most losses include some negative things you are glad you lost. Be honest with yourself and write them down.

   e. Every change has some advantages. Write them down. Focus on your advantages and make the best of them

6. Be gentle with yourself. Look for something beautiful in each day, and be thankful for all you receive. Do something kind for someone when you begin to feel better.

7. Move through your mourning into your new morning. Focus on creating a new beginning. See Mourning, Morning, p. 56.

Guilt

Critical Judge

Observer

Accused

1. Feeling GUILTY is like being a CRITICAL, harsh JUDGE and the ACCUSED and condemned at the same time. When you feel GUILTY, choose instead to be an OBSERVER, and move from the JUDGE'S bench to the OBSERVER'S bench.

   a. Be the OBSERVER. Put judgment aside. OBSERVE the situation, your behavior, and the behavior of the other people. Learn from the situation, and use it to improve yourself and your life.

   b. What are you aware of? What do you wish you did differently? Is there anything you now want to change? What action will you take?

   c. If you have difficulty taking the OBSERVER viewpoint, pretend a friend has the same situation, behavior, and feelings you have. How would you view the situation and feel about your friend? What suggestions would you have for your friend?

2. Do you use GUILT to punish and immobilize yourself, and feel as if you are in prison? GUILT can be like a prison door behind which you unconsciously hide other emotions you do not want to feel.

a. Ask yourself, "If I were not feeling GUILT, what other emotions would I feel?"

b. If it is anger, which it often is, see Anger, p. 14.

c. Do you immobilize yourself with GUILT because you fear going forward and making decisions and changes? If so, see Fear, p. 30, and Change, p. 19.

d. Use your thoughts, feelings, and behavior for yourself, not against yourself. Take action and go forward.

3. GUILT is based on the past. Do you feel GUILTY for things you did or did not do long ago, which you cannot change now? Do you think about them often and punish yourself with the memories?

a. Forgive and forget the things you wish you did differently. See Forgive, p. 31.

b. When you remember a painful memory and feel GUILTY, quickly replace it with a memory that makes you feel good about yourself.

4. GUILT is sometimes from not living up to childhood standards of parents, other people, and society.

a. Standards are conveyed as verbal and nonverbal messages. Remember and write down the messages. You may laugh at some and cry with others. Feel and express the emotions. See Expression, p. 22.

b. Now include, exclude, or change the messages.

c. Choose your own standards. Write a list of realistic, self-chosen adult standards and make them for the time and life you are living now.

d. Write new affirmations. See Affirmation, p. 12.

5. Is your GUILT from having realistic, self-chosen adult standards but not living up to them?

a. Do you want to improve your behavior in some specific ways?

b. Write down the changes you will make, and how, when, and where you will make them. And then make them.

6. GUILT is sometimes used to manipulate the behavior of children and adults.

a. If you manipulate others with GUILT, choose instead to state your feelings with "I feel _____" statements and ask for what you want.

b. When others use GUILT to manipulate you, tell them how you feel, ask them to tell you how they feel, and to directly ask you for what they want.

c. When others manipulate you with GUILT so you will take responsibility for them, state what is their responsibility and what is yours.

Happiness Is Balance

Activity	Inactivity
Exercise	Rest
Awake	Asleep
Speaking	Listening
Sound	Silence
Alone	Together
Giving	Receiving
Working	Playing
Spiritual	Physical
Mental	Emotional
Thinking	Feeling
Indoors	Outdoors
———	———
———	———
———	———

Are you HAPPY? Would you like to be HAPPIER?

1. Look at the words written opposite each other above, and think of how you are with each of those words.

    a. Next to each word write too little, too much, or BALANCED.

    b. Use the blank lines to fill in other things that are important to you and classify them the same way.

2. Experiencing too much of one side of the above words can be a reason for unhappiness. You may feel wonderful for awhile if you switch to the other side, but too much of that side and you probably will feel unhappy again.

3. What do you need more or less of to feel BALANCED and be HAPPIER?

4. Creating and maintaining BALANCE is a daily activity.

    a. What will you do today, this week, month, and year to BALANCE yourself and be HAPPIER?

    b. Write it down, and how, when, where, and for how long you will do it. And then do it!

37

Harmony

Harm

You are not in HARMONY when you are HARMING yourself or other people.

1. There are many ways you can HARM yourself and others, by what you do, and what you do not do. Physically, mentally, emotionally, spiritually, financially, and socially are some of the ways.

   a. List the ways you HARM yourself.

   b. List the ways you HARM others.

2. All behavior is an attempt to meet a need. HARMFUL behavior is an unhealthy attempt to meet a need.

   a. Read the list you wrote above. Think about the needs you may be trying to meet with your HARMFUL behaviors.

   b. Find healthy, HARMONIOUS ways to meet those needs.

3. Ask someone you know and respect to tell you how they think you HARM yourself and others.

4. HARMONY is having unity in the different parts of yourself.

a. Do you feel like a part of you wants to be good to you, and another part wants to do what HARMS you?

b. Create a dialogue between these two parts. Have each of them express their thoughts and feelings and say what they want.

c. Pretend there is a third part of you who speaks to the other two parts to mediate and work towards HARMONY.

d. Pretend a wise, loving being speaks and advises you on how to go from HARM to HARMONY.

5. HARMONY is having unity between you and other people, even though you are different.

a. Find and focus on ways you are the same.

b. View your differences as interesting, not threatening.

c. Accept other people as they are, and do not try to change them.

d. Be together with others for the length of time and to the degree you can be in HARMONY with yourself and with them.

6. What does being in HARMONY feel like to you?

a. Write about the feeling of HARMONY and the times you have felt HARMONIOUS.

b. Close your eyes and imagine being in HARMONY with yourself and others.

7. Recognize and appreciate the valuable person you are. When you do, you will not want to HARM yourself or allow other people to HARM you.

8. HARMING yourself can be a conscious or unconscious way to HARM other people when you feel angry with them. Instead, express your feelings in a healthy way. See Anger, p. 14.

9. What changes can you make to be in HARMONY with yourself and other people?

a. List the changes you will make.

b. Make an action plan and take action.

Higher Power

Low

1. A HIGHER POWER is a power you believe is greater than you believe you are. It can be in a religious, mythological, spiritual, metaphysical, or nature form or be formless.

   a. Do you believe in a HIGHER POWER?

   b. If you do, write a paragraph about your HIGHER POWER.

2. If you do not believe in a HIGHER POWER but want to believe, the following suggestions can be helpful.

   a. Write a paragraph about how you would like your HIGHER POWER to be, if you believed in one.

   b. Ask other people you respect and admire about their HIGHER POWER beliefs.

   c. Read biographies of great religious and spiritual people.

   d. Read religious and spiritual books and attend meetings and services.

   e. Sit quietly, close your eyes, and talk to a HIGHER POWER as if there may be one. Simply say, "I don't know if there is a HIGHER POWER. I want to believe there is. If you exist, please help me find and know you."

3. Explore your HIGHER POWER beliefs.

   a. What are your hopes or fears of believing in a HIGHER POWER?

   b. If you do not believe in a HIGHER POWER, what are your reasons for not believing in one?

   c. Are your HIGHER POWER beliefs your own beliefs or the beliefs of another person?

4. Have you gone through something you did not think you could get through? Did you feel as if you had help in an unknown way or from an unseen force?

5. Do you pray or speak to your HIGHER POWER?

   a. Do you believe your HIGHER POWER hears and answers you?

   b. If your HIGHER POWER gave you a message, what do you think the message would be?

6. What qualities and traits do you attribute to your HIGHER POWER? Write them down.

   a. Go through a day feeling and expressing the qualities and traits of your HIGHER POWER.

   b. Some people believe their highest and best self is like their HIGHER POWER. They seek to increasingly live and identify themselves with their HIGHER POWER.

   c. It is beautiful to see someone reflect and live the qualities of their HIGHER POWER. It is important not to make another person your HIGHER POWER.

7. Have you had an experience where you felt greater and more powerful than you ever believed you were? If so, write about it and read it often.

8. Feel your connection to your HIGHER POWER.

   a. Have a symbol that evokes your HIGHER POWER feelings. Close your eyes and imagine you see, touch, or hear your symbol.

   b. Have sounds, words, or music that help you feel your HIGHER POWER connection.

9. Sacred places can help you feel close to your HIGHER POWER.

   a. Have a sacred place shared by other people who believe as you do. Be there often.

   b. Have a sacred place in your home. It can be a tiny corner or an entire room. Include your favorite sacred pictures and objects.

   c. Have a quiet, peaceful, sacred place in nature.

   d. When you want to be in one of your sacred places and cannot be there, close your eyes and imagine you are there.

10. If you could be in the presence of your HIGHER POWER, what would that be like? Imagine it now.

Hope

Strong Desire
Expectation Of Fulfillment

1. Think about everything you HOPED for in the past that became a reality.

   a. Write everything down and leave blank lines between each item.

   b. Write down on the blank lines what you did to make them be realities.

2. What do you HOPE for now?

   a. Write a list of what you HOPE for and leave a blank line between each item.

   b. Write down on the blank lines what you will do to make your HOPES become realities.

   c. Choose one of the things you HOPE for and make it a primary goal.

d. Create a "HOPEFUL Poster." Find, cut out, and paste words and pictures that represent what you HOPE for on a large sheet of paper or poster board. Place it where you see it often and fill yourself with the good feelings of having your HOPES be realities.

e. When a HOPE becomes a reality, put a big star next to that item and write THANK YOU in large letters.

f. Take each item on your list and write down all of its specific details. Next, write it out in the form of a request and add, "This or something better for the highest and best good of all concerned." End by writing a thank you as if it already occurred. Date and put it in a special place, such as a spiritual book or special container.

g. Write THANK YOU across your requests when they are fulfilled. Keep them in an envelope marked "Fulfilled HOPES." Read and remember them when you need HOPE in the future.

h. Visualize your HOPES being realities. See Visualize, p. 65.

3. Prepare yourself to have your HOPES become realities.

a. Are you ready? What inner and outer preparations do you need to make? If you do not know, imagine what you HOPE for is already a reality. From that viewpoint know what you can do to prepare yourself.

b. Make a list of what you will do and then do it.

4. Confront your concerns and fears of having your HOPES be realities.

a. What do you think you would lose? What changes do you fear you would have to make? What new things that you fear doing, or do not want to do, would you have to do?

b. See suggestions for Fear, p. 30.

5. Pretend it is the future and your HOPES are realities.

a. Write a letter of encouragement and advice from your future self, who is living that reality, to your present self, who is HOPING to live it.

b. Give yourself an "act as if" experience. Go through a day pretending you have what you want.

c. Children love to pretend, especially when someone pretends with them. Give your inner child a "Playful Pretend Partner." Together, playfully pretend what you HOPE for is already a reality.

Hugs

Ughs

1. Physical touch increases feelings of emotional, mental, and physical well-being.

2. Give yourself a HUG anywhere and anytime you need one.

   a. It can be a great big HUG with your arms wrapped tightly around yourself, as your hands lovingly squeeze and caress your arms and shoulders.

   b. It can be a small, discrete HUG so only you know you are HUGGING yourself. Gently hold one hand in the other hand, hold your arms closely at your sides, and give your hands and arms a little squeeze.

   c. Feel the nurturing and love you can give to yourself.

3. Ask someone if you can give them a HUG.

4. Ask someone to HUG you.

5. Have a group HUG with three or more people.

6. Close your eyes and imagine you are with someone you love, who also loves you. Pretend you are HUGGING each other. Physically and emotionally feel the HUG.

Humor

Do you want More HUMOR?

1. Remember the funniest experience you have ever had.

    a. Fill yourself again with the feelings you had then.

    b. Tell someone about the experience.

2. HUMOR is an attitude.

    a. As you go through your daily experiences, adopt a HUMOROUS attitude.

    b. Ask yourself frequently, "If I looked at this HUMOROUSLY, how HUMOROUS could it be?" Enjoy the HUMOROUS possibilities.

3. HUMOR is an action.

    a. Think of a HUMOROUS surprise for someone. Take action and make it a reality.

    b. Make plans and be with people who are HUMOROUS and fun.

    c. Purchase a book of HUMOR. Read it whenever you want to laugh.

    d. Choose and watch HUMOROUS movies and videos, and listen to HUMOROUS tapes.

    e. Choose a HUMOROUS stuffed animal or puppet that makes you laugh. Place it where you see it often.

Insight

Turn the DARKNESS of confusion into the light of INSIGHT through mental activity and mental inactivity.

1. What is the problem, or stated positively, the challenge, for which you need INSIGHT? Focus your mind on your challenge.

    a. Sit quietly and think about your challenge. Write down everything you are aware of. Read what you have written.

    b. Write down all your alternatives and the pros and cons of each.

    c. Decide what action you will take.

2. Take your mind off the challenge.

    a. Do something that requires your total involvement in the present.

    b. Totally involve yourself in a physical activity, such as a sport, house cleaning, or gardening.

    c. Later focus on the challenge again and be aware of any new INSIGHT.

Darkness

3. Get inner information by decreasing the activity of your mind.

    a. Learn to meditate. See Meditate, p. 54.

    b. Sit quietly. Close your eyes. Breathe fully and deeply. When you inhale say to yourself, "I am," and when you exhale say to yourself, "relaxed."

    c. When your mind and body begin to relax, imagine you are in a peaceful, beautiful meadow. Pretend you can see, touch, and smell the lovely flowers, feel the grass beneath your feet, hear the birds, feel the breeze, and see the sky. Relax in the peace.

    d. If your mind begins to wander, bring it back to your imagined peaceful place.

    e. Simply sit in the silence. During or after calming your mind, you may have new INSIGHT.

4. You may have INSIGHT from a dream, upon awakening, or during the next day by following these suggestions.

    a. After you go to bed take a few long, slow, deep breaths.

    b. When you feel relaxed, state the question you want answered and then go to sleep.

    c. Repeat daily until you have your answer.

Jealous? See

- Present Facts
- Self-Worth
- Personal Power

Jealousy

1. JEALOUSY is fear of losing what you have, or of someone else having what you want. It is a belief that something is lacking in yourself or in what you want. It often stems from the past, when you didn't get enough of what you wanted because there was not enough, or it was given to someone else. You may have believed it was because something was wrong with you.

2. When you feel JEALOUS, ask yourself two questions.

   a. "Based on my emotions, what is my mind telling me?"

   b. "Am I reacting to PRESENT FACTS, to memories from my past, or to fears I have created and projected into my future?"

c. And then use your mind to focus on the PRESENT FACTS.

3. JEALOUSY is often an emotional over reaction. You may feel the way you do, know you are over reacting, and be upset for feeling that way.

   a. Acknowledge and accept what you feel.

   b. Express your feelings to a caring, non-judgmental person and be compassionate with yourself.

4. If your feelings involve another person, you may want to talk to that person.

   a. Express your feelings, perceptions, and thoughts and take responsibility for them. Use "I" statements. Do not verbally attack the other person.

   b. Ask the other person to express their perceptions, feelings, and thoughts.

   c. Ask for what you want, and ask what they want.

   d. Attempt to work out a win/win solution.

5. If JEALOUSY is intense, familiar, and frequent, you probably are responding more to past emotions than to PRESENT FACTS. Are your present feelings and circumstances similar to a prior time?

   a. Knowing they are may help you separate the past emotions from the present situation so you can focus on the PRESENT FACTS.

   b. If knowing this does not help, go back to the earlier time and express the feelings you did not express then. See Expression, p. 22.

   c. Close your eyes and in your imagination recreate that earlier situation the way you wanted it to be.

   d. Give yourself what you wanted in your imagination, in reality, or in a symbolic form.

   e. Find out your beliefs from those experiences and write affirmations to change them. See Affirmation, p. 12.

6. JEALOUSY can be from low SELF-WORTH and not using your PERSONAL POWER. Do you give POWER for your SELF-WORTH and resources to another person, and want to possess and control their feelings and behavior?

   a. Value and appreciate the special and unique person you are. Praise yourself. See Praise, p. 61.

   b. Choose something you want that you can give to yourself, and give yourself as much of it as you want.

   c. Use your PERSONAL POWER to control yourself and your resources, and not to control someone else.

   d. Choose a goal you can work towards and reach. Validate and reward yourself when you reach it.

Joy
&
Love

Do you want to feel JOY?

1. JOY and LOVE often are together. Not all of the time you feel LOVE will you feel JOY, but most of the time you feel JOY, you will feel LOVE.

   a. Do what you LOVE to do. Make a list of what you LOVE doing, and next to each item write when you last did it, and when you will do it again.

   b. Be with the people you LOVE to be with. How much of your daily, weekly, and yearly time are you with the people you LOVE?

   c. Be where you LOVE to be. Do you feel more JOYFUL in some places than in others? How much time are you in your JOYFUL places?

2. JOY is a feeling of fullness, of being fulfilled in the moment. Take a "JOYFUL Journey" back through your life to all of your JOYFUL times.

   a. Write down your JOYFUL experiences. You may have many, or you may have to search to find a few. Remember all the details, no matter how insignificant they seem.

   b. JOYFULLY experience those memories now.

   c. Find the similarities in your JOYFUL experiences to learn what most helps you feel your inner JOY.

   d. Tell someone your "JOYFUL Journey" memories.

3. JOY is total involvement and satisfaction in the present.

   a. JOY is having your body, emotions, and mind in the present as you experience through your senses. See Present, p. 62.

   b. Be outside in nature. Nature's changes and surprises often demand total involvement in the present.

   c. Do something playful with young children, who totally involve themselves and others in the present.

   d. Do something you have not done before. See Hi!, p. 53.

4. JOY is making fulfilling choices.

   a. Make choices for your own fulfillment and happiness, not only for outer reward, status, or to fulfill other people's expectations.

   b. Fulfilling choices help you express who you truly are. Does your work, home, relationships, and leisure activities express who you truly are? If not, what changes will you make so they will?

5. JOY is often felt during child-like play.

   a. What did you LOVE to do when you were a child? Remember your favorite forms of play and play them now. If you can not, what was the essence of the playful experience? Give it to yourself in another form.

   b. Play on a playground. Slide down a slide. Ride on a merry-go-round and swing.

   c. Walk barefooted in the rain. Splash in puddles.

   d. Use crayons, markers, or finger paints, and playfully express yourself on paper with eyes closed and then with eyes opened.

   e. Go to a toy store and discover the many toys. Choose and buy one for yourself.

   f. Enjoy spontaneous, unplanned play.

   g. Feel the joy of magical, pretend play with a playful partner. Use your imagination to be anyone, anywhere you wish to be.

6. Make JOYFUL experiences a priority in your life.

7. JOY can be felt from setting and reaching a goal, especially if you did something that helped you expand beyond who you thought you were.

   a. Set a goal.

   b. Make an action plan and go forward to reach your goal.

Lonely

Alone

Do You Feel LONELY or ALONE?

1. Having a balance between being ALONE and being with other people can make the difference between feeling LONELY and ALONE. Balance the time you are ALONE and with others.

2. Sometimes LONELY means feeling empty and wanting another person to fill the emptiness. The ALONE person can often fill his or her emptiness, can feel full, and may want another person with whom to share that fullness.

   a. Think about, write down, and act on those things you enjoy. Fill yourself up.

   b. Find ways to fill yourself up while being with other people.

3. A way to move from feeling LONELY to ALONE is to perceive and use being ALONE in a positive way. Write down the advantages of being ALONE.

4. If being by yourself is new for you, think of what you wanted to do and didn't do when you were with another person and do it now. See New, p. 57.

5. LONELINESS can result from a lack of emotional intimacy. Share your inner feelings and thoughts with another person.

Love

1. LOVE can be expressed in four major ways. They are touching, telling, giving, and doing.

2. LOVE can be conditional, "I LOVE you if," or unconditional, "I LOVE you for being who you are."

3. LOVE yourself.

   a. Fill your life with people, experiences, and things you LOVE.

   b. Do something LOVING for yourself every day. Each night write down what you did that day.

   c. If you have difficulty LOVING yourself, close your eyes and think of someone who LOVES you. It can be from the present or long ago. Fill yourself with that LOVE.

   d. Write down everything you LOVE about yourself.

4. LOVE others.

   a. Make today an "I LOVE you day." Surprise people you LOVE by expressing your LOVE for them in a special way.

   b. Ask someone how they would like you to express your LOVE, and then LOVINGLY express it that way.

   c. Do something LOVING for someone and remain anonymous.

   d. Express unconditional LOVE for someone who needs it.

5. Be LOVED by others.

   a. Place pictures of those who LOVE you where you can see them often. Fill yourself with their LOVE.

   b. Make it a priority to be with people who LOVE you. Have quality time with them often.

   c. Ask someone who LOVES you to express their LOVE for you in the way you want to receive it.

6. Be LOVE.

   a. Imagine you are LOVE in a physical form.

   b. Go through a day seeing with eyes of LOVE, listening with ears of LOVE, speaking with words of LOVE, and touching with hands of LOVE.

Hi!

Low

Are you feeling LOW? Want to feel HIGH?

1. Experiencing something new often brings a HIGH. Make a decision to have a "HI!" day. Choose a new way to do things from the time you wake up, until you go to bed.
2. What do you want to say "HI!" to? What new feelings, things, people, places, events, and experiences do you want in your life? Write them down.
3. Write down what you will do to give yourself what you want, and how, when, and where you will do it. Begin now to say "HI!" to the new.

Meditate

1. MEDITATION is beneficial for the body, mind, and emotions. It can help you relax and reduce stress. It has many positive effects and no side effects.

2. MEDITATE daily, preferably twice a day for ten to twenty minutes, morning and night.

   a. Sit in a quiet, comfortable place. Close your eyes. Breathe fully and deeply.

   b. Choose a word or sound that feels relaxing and good to you, such as peace, aahhh, or a spiritual word.

   c. Silently, slowly, and gently repeat your word.

   d. Don't be concerned about your thoughts. When you have thoughts, let them be like trains that come into your awareness and pass by. If you find you have gone off with one of them, gently bring yourself back to repeating your word.

3. To experience the greatest benefits from MEDITATION, make MEDITATION a priority. Make and keep a commitment with yourself to MEDITATE daily.

4. You may want to do focused breathing prior to MEDITATION, or you can do it any time when you want to relax.

a. Breathe long, slow, deep breaths. Breathe in through your nose, and out through your mouth.

b. Focus your mind on your rhythmic inhales and exhales. Say to yourself as you inhale, "I am," and as you exhale, "Relaxed."

c. You can calm your emotions by making your exhales twice as long as your inhales. Count slowly as you inhale, and then exhale to a count double that number.

d. Making a sound, such as a long "aaaahhhh," as you exhale can help you release tension.

e. You may begin to yawn. Good! This is a sign you are relaxing.

f. Counting as you breathe for a certain number of breaths, such as three or seven, or until you feel relaxed and want to stop, may help you keep your mind focused on your breathing.

5. The following progressive relaxation can be done prior to MEDITATION, or whenever you want to be relaxed.

a. Sit in a comfortable chair if you plan to follow your progressive relaxation with MEDITATION. Otherwise lie down or sit up, whichever you choose.

b. Begin at the top of your head and progress down to your feet. Relax a section of your body at a time by tightening, tensing, and holding the tightness and tension for a short time, and then relaxing and letting the tension go.

c. For example, tighten and tense your scalp, forehead, cheeks, eyes, ears, mouth, and neck. Hold the tension and then release, relax, and let the tension go. Do this slowly for your entire body.

d. Allow your body to relax into the surface beneath you. Feel that it is being held up and that there is nothing you need to do. Simply enjoy the feeling of relaxation.

6. The following are two MEDITATIVE visualization exercises that can be used after the focused breathing and/or the progressive relaxation to more fully relax. You can record and listen to them, have someone slowly read them to you, or memorize them.

a. Imagine you see or touch a large inflated balloon. Be aware of what color it is. Breathe long, slow, deep breaths. With each exhale the balloon slowly deflates and you slowly relax until it is completely deflated, and you are relaxed.

b. Pretend you are standing on a hillside overlooking a beautiful meadow. Imagine you feel the warmth of the noon sun and a gentle breeze. See a nearby path and begin walking down the hillside. Step by step walk deeper and deeper down the path into the meadow. Hear the birds chirping and the stream flowing nearby. See the colors of lovely flowers and smell their scent. Feel the long, soft, green grass beneath your body as you lie down to rest. When you feel rested, stand up and pick some flowers as you begin walking back up the path. At the top of the hill reach and stretch your arms up into the air. Look up into the blue sky, take a long, slow, deep breath, and say to yourself, "I am relaxed and renewed." Slowly and gently, when you are ready, open your eyes and bring your awareness back to your surroundings.

Mourning   Morning

Are you in MOURNING and want a new MORNING?

1. MOURNING is grieving a loss. MORNING is a gain of a new beginning.

2. An ending is also a beginning, and a beginning is an ending of something else.

3. Changes have endings and beginnings. A change can be a chosen change or an unchosen change. Most changes have gains and losses.

   a. Loss and MOURNING are usually felt first in an unchosen change, and the gain and MORNING are felt later.

   b. The gain is more often felt first with a chosen change, and loss and MOURNING are felt later.

   c. With most changes you will go back and forth some between MOURNING and MORNING. Knowing this is normal can help you accept your feelings.

4. Are you MOURNING a loss and an ending? Feel and express your emotions. See Sadness, p. 64, and Grief, p. 33.

5. Give yourself a beginning of something new and different, a new MORNING!

   a. Write a list of what you would like to do that you haven't yet done, and what you have done that you want to do again.

   b. Research and find new possibilities for meeting your needs, enriching your life, and discovering your inner potentials. Take action!

   c. Make certain you have a MORNING each day by adding something new to your day, no matter how small it might be.

6. Move through your MOURNING and live your new MORNING.

The News

Knew   New

1. Do you need to go forward from what you KNEW to the NEW? Is it a big step for you, and are you frightened to take the step?

2. Have you already taken the first step and feel caught between what you KNEW and the NEW? Do you sometimes want to go forward and live the NEW, and other times want to go back and live what you KNEW?

3. Do you feel upset to leave what you KNEW behind you? Take what benefited you from your past, and bring it with you as you go forward.

   a. You may not be able to bring the actual form with you, but be able to bring the essence, gifts, and learning lessons from the form.

b. Write a list of what you are bringing with you from the KNEW to the NEW.

4. Are there people, things, and experiences you cannot bring with you to the NEW? See Release, p. 63.

5. What emotions do you feel? See suggestions for your emotions, such as Fear, p. 30, Sadness, p. 64, or Anger, p. 14.

6. Did you have to go from what you KNEW to the NEW and did not want to?

   a. If so, do you feel frightened and powerless? Discover the areas and ways you do have choice and control.

   b. If you cannot change the circumstances, change yourself in the circumstances.

7. If going forward to the NEW is difficult for you, and you have a choice, go to the NEW slowly, one area of your life at a time.

8. What do you want to do that you haven't yet done?

   a. Let yourself dream the possible, and what seems to be the impossible. Make a list and write it all down.

   b. Write a fairytale of how you want your NEW life to be.

9. Imagine the NEW.

   a. Visualize yourself being where you want to be, and doing what you want to do. See Visualize, p. 65.

   b. Imagine yourself standing happily and securely in the NEW, with a smile on your face as the sun shines above.

10. Take action to make your hopes and dreams become your realities.

11. Turn your fear into excitement, and feel your excitement pull you forward to the NEW.

Pieces   Peace

Do you want to be in one PEACE?

1. PEACE comes from bringing your PIECES into one PEACE. You can do this physically, mentally, emotionally, and spiritually.

2. One of the fastest ways to feel PEACE anytime, anywhere, is through deep breathing.

   a. Breathe long, slow, deep breaths. Focus your mind on your rhythmic inhales and exhales. You may begin to yawn. Good! This is a sign you are relaxing.

   b. Make your exhales twice as long as your inhales to calm your emotions.

3. Relax your body, quiet your mind, and calm your emotions.

   a. Do physical activity and then inactivity. Examples are taking a walk in nature and then sitting in a peaceful place outdoors, or gardening or house cleaning and then leisurely taking a warm bath.

   b. Do a progressive relaxation. Begin at the top of your head and progress down to your feet. Alternately tighten and tense and then relax a section of your body at a time until your entire body is relaxed.

c. Meditate daily. See Meditate, p. 54.

4. Love and kindness bring PIECES into one PEACE within yourself and with other people.

   a. Do something loving and kind for yourself.

   b. Do something loving and kind for someone to bring PEACE where there has been conflict.

5. PEACE is having no inner battles. If you believe one way and live another, you will be at war within yourself.

   a. Think about and write down what is most important to you. Does your life express this?

   b. If not, take action to make your daily life express your priorities.

6. Forgiveness is important for PEACE. Inner and outer battles often mean you need to forgive yourself and others. See Forgive, p. 31.

7. Acceptance of yourself and others is important for PEACE.

   a. Write down "What I need to accept in myself," and "What I need to change in myself," and then take action to do so.

   b. Write down "What I need to stop trying to change in other people," and "What I need to accept in other people." Acceptance is easier if you do not allow their behavior to hurt you.

   c. PEACE with others is easier if you perceive and accept their differences as interesting, not threatening.

   d. Think of someone you are not at PEACE with. Find and concentrate on how you are the same. Focus on how you agree, not on how you disagree.

8. Having and living your own spiritual beliefs and practices can be helpful for PEACE. See Higher Power, p. 40.

9. Create your own "PEACEFUL Places."

   a. Have an indoor "PEACEFUL Place." It can be a tiny corner or an entire room. Include your favorite PEACEFUL objects and pictures. Make it comfortable.

   b. Have a "PEACEFUL Place" in nature. Be there often.

   c. Have a "PEACEFUL Place" in your imagination. Imagine and include everything that makes you feel PEACEFUL. See, touch, smell, hear, taste, and feel it. When you need to feel PEACE, close your eyes and breathe long, slow, deep breaths. Imagine you are in your special place.

10. Be outdoors in nature for at least a short time every day. Be in silence for part of that time. Use your senses to see, hear, smell, touch, and feel your surroundings.

Praise — Raise

Giving and receiving PRAISE
RAISES feelings of love and self-esteem.

1. PRAISE yourself.

   a. Sit quietly and think of what you like about your-self. If this is difficult, think of someone who loves you, either from the present or long ago. Feel their love. Imagine they tell you what they like about you, and then think of what you like about your-self.

   b. Make a list of the things you like about yourself.

   c. Write a letter to yourself. Begin with "Dear (your name), I PRAISE you for ...," and write everything that comes to your mind.

   d. Tell someone what you like about yourself. PRAISE yourself for who you are and what you do.

P.RAISE

2. PRAISE other people.

   a. Tell others what you like about them. Be aware of how you feel about yourself when you verbally PRAISE others.

   b. Write a sincere letter of PRAISE to someone.

   c. Have a "Day of PRAISE." Find something to PRAISE in everyone you meet. Verbalize the PRAISE.

3. Receive PRAISE.

   a. Ask someone to tell you what they like about you.

   b. Accept PRAISE without feeling you need to return the PRAISE.

   c. Remember PRAISE you received in the past and again feel RAISED by that PRAISE.

4. Begin a "PRAISE Partnership" with someone. Speak with them at least three times a week. Take turns PRAISING yourself, giv-ing PRAISE, and receiving PRAISE.

Present

Be PRESENT.

1. Make a conscious effort to be aware of your thoughts for the next hour. Say to yourself, "PAST, PRESENT, or FUTURE," as you become aware of the time frame of a thought. It is normal to have thoughts of PAST and FUTURE, but happiness is having the greatest percentage of thoughts in the PRESENT, so it truly is a gift you give to yourself.

2. Experience your PRESENT through your senses.

   a. Close your eyes. Take long, slow, deep breaths. Inhale and exhale fully. Listen. Hear all the sounds.

   b. Take another long, slow, deep breath. Slowly open your eyes. Look around and see things you may not have seen before.

   c. Close your eyes. Take long, slow, deep breaths. Smell the scents around you as you inhale.

   d. Take a long, slow, deep breath. With eyes closed, touch and feel one hand against your other hand. Then feel your face, clothing, and objects within reach.

   e. Choose something to taste, and have it in your hands. Close your eyes. Take a long, slow, deep breath and slowly taste.

3. When you are aware you are not in the PRESENT choose a sense, such as sight, and say to yourself, "I see ____." Fill in the blank with what you are seeing at that moment. Randomly switch back and forth in the same way with all your senses until you are fully aware of your PRESENT.

4. When you are aware you are in the PAST or FUTURE in your thoughts, say to yourself, "I am PRESENT," and breathe fully and deeply.

Release To Re-Lease!

1. Do you need to RELEASE?

   a. Do you hold onto feelings, thoughts, people, events, times, places, and things that are familiar from your past? Do you need to RELEASE them to experience the new? The old may have been happy and fulfilling or unhappy and unrewarding. Do you hold onto the old because it was known and fear going forward to the unknown of the new?

   b. What do you need to RELEASE? Make a list of what, how, when, and where you will RELEASE. You can write it down on Write It Out, p. 68. It is possible to RELEASE an item and keep the good you received from it.

   c. RELEASE what you are ready to RELEASE. What can you do to prepare yourself to RELEASE what you are not yet ready to RELEASE?

   d. After you RELEASE an item, boldly write RE-LEASED across that item.

2. Give yourself a "New LEASE on Life."

   a. What do you want your "New LEASE On Life" to include? Write a list of the new feelings, thoughts, people, events, times, places, and things you want. Choose one thing that is easy for you to give to yourself and give it to yourself now.

   b. Write down what you will do to bring in the new, and how, when, and where you will do it.

   c. Create a "New LEASE on Life" poster. Write, draw, cut out, and paste pictures and words that represent what you want on a large sheet of paper or poster board. Place it where you see it often. When you give yourself one of the new things, write THANK YOU in large letters across the picture or word.

   d. Create a "New LEASE on Life" scroll. Write "I, _____(your name), do hereby give a NEW LEASE ON LIFE to myself on _____(date)." Signed _____ Witnessed _____

   e. Ask someone to be a "RELEASING Partner," and to witness your scroll signing. Speak with them at least twice a week. Tell them what you have RELEASED and what new things you have given to yourself.

Sadness Out

Love &
Kindness In

Feeling SAD? Get the SADNESS out, and LOVE and KINDNESS in.

1. Express your hurt, pain, and disappointment without judging yourself.

    a. Cry it out, speak it out, or write it out.

    b. Afterwards, do something LOVING and KIND for yourself. If you do not know what to do, think of what you would do for a SAD child or a SAD friend, and do that for yourself.

2. Ask someone to be with you as you express your SADNESS.

    a. Ask them to simply LOVE and listen to you. Tell them to be silent, not to give you advice, and not to try to solve your problems.

    b. You might want to ask them to give you a hug, to hold your hand, or to let you cry on their shoulder, if you both feel comfortable doing so. Being touched in a LOVING, nurturing, non-threatening way can sometimes help SADNESS be expressed.

    c. Afterwards ask them to do something LOVING and KIND for you, perhaps to rub your back or to get you something to eat.

    d. Do something LOVING and KIND for yourself.

Visualize

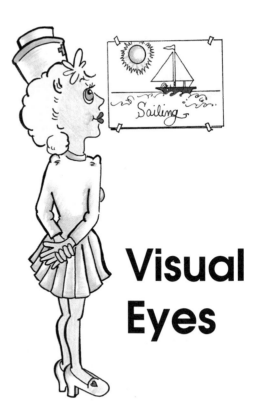

Visual Eyes

VISUALIZE with your VISUAL EYES.

1. What do you want? Write it down.
2. VISUALIZE with your inner eyes.

   a. Sit quietly. Close your eyes. Breathe fully and deeply. When you inhale say to yourself, "I am," and when you exhale say to yourself, "relaxed."

   b. When you feel your mind and body relax, VISUALIZE a large, blank, white movie screen. Create your own movie of what you want on your movie screen.

   c. See where you are, what you are doing, what you have, who is with you, and how happy you are as you have what you want.

   d. You are the script writer, the director, the producer, and the actress or actor.

3. VISUALIZE with your outer eyes.

   a. Find and cut out pictures and words that represent what you want and paste them on paper.

   b. Place them where you see them often. Fill yourself with the good feelings of having what you want.

4. Write down and begin the necessary actions to make your VISUALIZATION a reality.

Whole

Hole

Do you want to feel WHOLE?

1. Difficult emotional experiences in childhood can cause emotional difficulties as an adult.

2. When you have emotionally similar experiences as an adult, you may feel like you are in an emotional HOLE. You feel the emotions from the present, and may feel unexpressed emotions and unmet needs from the childhood experience.

3. The following questions are clues to help you know if your emotions are mainly from the present experience or more of an emotional reaction from the past.

   a. Do you feel too much emotion?

   b. Do you feel too little emotion?

   c. Have you felt this way before?

   d. Do you feel stuck, powerless, and helpless?

4. Draw a line of your life to find your emotional HOLES. You can do this alone or with a partner. Have one person do the process and the other be the loving, listening friend. Later switch roles. Do not give advice or try to solve each other's problems.

   a. Take some time to quietly reflect on your life from birth up to the present time.

   b. Use blank sheets of paper and draw a line that represents your life. Beginning with your birth, draw and write in the major events. Also include seemingly minor events that had an emotional impact. Draw the line lower or higher to indicate your emotional highs and lows.

c. When you finish, place the line of your life so you can see all of it at one time.

d. Find the places and events where you feel emotional and incomplete to identify your emotional HOLES.

5. The following are steps you can take to complete your experiences and help yourself feel more emotionally WHOLE. It can be helpful to have a psychological professional guide you. If your emotions are more than moderate, it is advised that you seek professional help and not do the steps alone.

   a. Feel the emotions.

   b. Complete the interrupted expression. Express the emotions now you did not express then. Use the suggestions for your emotions, such as Sadness, p. 64, Anger, p. 14, or Fear, p. 30, so you will know how to express them in a way that will not hurt you or another person.

   c. What was your need that wasn't met then? Meet your need now in actuality, in imagination, or in another form.

   d. What are your messages, beliefs, decisions, behaviors, and patterns from those experiences? Write them down. Write positive new messages, beliefs, and decisions on your life line. Write new affirmations. See Affirmation, p 12.

6. Emotional HOLES usually contain unfinished business with other people. Sentence completions are a way to finish the unfinished business.

   a. Write letters to people with whom you have unfinished business. This is for your benefit, not to send to the other person unless it is wise to do so. Express your true feelings.

   b. What I need to say to you is _____.

   c. I feel _____.

d. I resent _____.

e. I regret _____.

f. I want _____.

g. I let go of _____.

h. I keep _____.

i. I appreciate _____.

j. I say goodbye to _____.

k. I say hello to _____.

7. Express the emotions you feel when you write the above letters by using the suggestions for that emotion.

8. See Forgive and Forget, p. 31.

9. HOLES are potential power spots. They usually contain memories, emotions, unmet needs, dreams, heart's desires, and the potentials and personal power to help you move forward to greater fulfillment.

10. What did you discover about yourself and your life?

    a. Write down your new awarenesses.

    b. Your experiences, even the difficult ones, helped you develop necessary skills, positive qualities, and admirable traits. Next to the events on your life line write the benefits you received from them.

    c. What were your happy discoveries?

    d. Did you discover any dreams and heart's desires?

    e. Is there anything you want to do differently?

    f. What will you do to move forward to greater fulfillment and WHOLENESS?

11. Acknowledge and validate yourself for all you are, and what you have experienced, learned, and done.

Write It Out

Right It Out

Information

For information about Victoria Ann Johnson's seminars,
Please write to:

Victoria Ann Johnson, M. A.
P. O. Box 1966
Boca Raton, Florida 33432